Water Shedding

poems by

Beth Konkoski

Finishing Line Press
Georgetown, Kentucky

Water Shedding

ACKNOWLEDGMENTS

Pamplemousse: "Linger;" "Agitating Beauty"
Saranac Review: "Fragile Do Not Drop"
The Potomac Review: "Watching Laziness"
The Aurorean: "August in the Raspberry Patch"
vox poetica: "When I Was Eleven"
Gargoyle : "Sleep-Away Camp;" "Winter Rounds;" "North on 81"
Loch Raven Review: "Reincarnate"
Steamticket : "A Wardrobe of Stolen Dreams"
TEXTure: "First Words"
The Clementine Poetry Review: "Aubade;" "Balance Beam"
Blast Furnace: "Flood"
Courtship of Winds: "Now I See the Drawing You Made"
Write Time Write Place: "The Heron"
Gyroscope Review: "Timing;" "Gathering"
Boston Accent Literary Magazine: "After Rain"
Barbaric Yawp: "Altered Plans"
Noticing the Splash chapbook: "In the Dammed River"

Publisher: Leah Maines
Editor: Christen Kincaid
Cover Art: Linda Konkoski
Author Photo: Claire Bates
Cover Design: Leah Huete

Printed in the USA on acid-free paper.
Order online: www.finishinglinepress.com
also available on amazon.com

Author inquiries and mail orders:
Finishing Line Press
P. O. Box 1626
Georgetown, Kentucky 40324
U. S. A.

Table of Contents

For Jim, Sam, and Claire because I love you.
Thanks for all the ways you fill up my life.

Up on the watershed
Standing at the fork in the road
You can stand there and agonize
'Til your agony's your heaviest load

—The Indigo Girls, "Watershed"

Linger

We could perch on the details
of this near end. How I
have worn you
as my skin for decades,
let every sense curve
toward a blossom
or fruit of your choice.
Burning any fringe
or edge you don't like,
I beg to fit in your chosen
mold, to slide like a wedge
of orange between your teeth.
Steps without you
are shards or ribbons,
weeds, cardboard boxes
thrown in my path.
And I have forgotten
the muscles used for lifting.

Fragile, Do Not Drop

On a good day I sense I'm breathing through glass,
not shards cutting deep, just a dome of fine glass.

I can almost press my hand to the edges,
but then fall, an insect captured beneath glass.

As a child I sat for hours in church,
afraid that my sins would leak out, staining glass.

For holidays we graced and passed neatly to the right;
our manners stored deep in the crystals of glass.

The storm freezes us hard in a place we call love
until morning shines through silver-frosted glass.

Nobody told me how fragile boredom is—
a porcelain smile now swept away glass.

Not empty or full, no half-liquid to inspect.
I am afraid of space outside the glass.

Mirrors and their half-lives call out and move past;
I tap down the walls, blank safety in my glass.

Watching Laziness

Pablo Neruda says
high up in the pines
laziness appears naked.

So we go outside
to gawk, our hair
in oily strands needing
a wash, and wonder
how she climbed
to where she sways
in the wind.
When did she undress,
this arboreal
debutante of sloth?
Has she always been
without covering,
born high in the trees
to look down
as we plod along and fail
to hear the bristly
symphony of pine needles?
We would join her
if we could manage
the climb, or hang
safely once we arrived.
Instead we sit
watching her freedom,
humbled by the intensity
that true
laziness requires.

August in the Raspberry Patch

She steps with me into the patch
afraid of scratches,
her mouth awaits
red, expects sweet
she has tasted but never picked.
Into thickets
of green, shifting
sunlight, lifting
leaves, a slow search for the secret
simple moment,
Is it ready?
She pulls at me,
points into pickered shadows;
I must say *no*
too pink, but here,
reaching with fear
she threads her way in with the bees,
touches but leaves
a naked stem,
berry fallen
among the roots
and dust.

When I Was Eleven

Summer boredom hit
that first Tuesday,
the allotted hours between
meals and swims long as a circle
of rosary beads.
By evening we prowled the cage
of time until our parents
heaved us into the blackness
letting fireflies and street lights
guide us.
Find something to do.
In a few years they would
not turn us loose so easily,
wishing us back to nights
of safe summer boredom.
On banana seat bikes
we pedaled air, erect,
on balance, riding no hands
as we took the hill
full speed racing.
Indifferent to cars,
we reached for the black shuddery
promise of trees
holding hands above us.

Sleep-Away Camp

I have driven him to this camp
where the trees touch hands above our heads
and must leave him without bread crumbs,
a cell phone. While he's not at all scared

or sad, *Got it Mom*, I must watch
as his prepositions shift—away,
beyond, out of state. I almost
call him back to me, but think instead

of the stepmother and her choice.
Did Hansel and Gretel's father leash
them tightly to a tree, his fear
thick as weed spores, his grip cutting off

the wind of each day, so intent
on witch danger that he did not show
them truffle growth or creek bed paths
leading home? Locking gates and closing

windows, we cage them with safety
and wonder when they do not flourish.
So I turn toward the car, whisper
a prayer, and wave as he disappears.

The Light of Day

We are not the mulberry
acid of tongues
spreading hate where it
can take root.

We are not bones
thumping loud mistakes
in concert
with the wind.

We are not time
trudging in clogs
through the mud
of all days.

We are not what we avoid,
what we keep hidden,
until a child's heart
reminds us.

Family Dinner

The scrape of our knives cutting
roasted pork makes each of us cringe.
We taste the sawdust minutes
of silence each night, as our jaws
lock and unlock to chew and pulp
broccoli steamed nearly colorless.
Too many screeches of metal
on glazed plates, the fine lines
wear to black over time and this
ritual which we have held to
with the force and desperation of one
clutching a raft in the swells
of a cannibal sea, accomplishes
nothing. But we continue unraveling
these evenings, pretend we are lucky
to have one another.

Reincarnate

In my next life, if I get one, I will be the damsel
in need of a prince and a horse or maybe
an entire army to relieve my distress. Enough
of this equality and independence. Tired
as Sleeping Beauty and too skilled in the scrubbing
arts, the serving and hauling required of the maid
to an evil relative, I hang on the cusp of some
prince's arrival. My problem: I take too much
satisfaction in moving the couch myself. I am
only now, as fifty looms and the prospect of a hero
to free me shrinks, seeing how furniture moved
by the biceps and strain of another might conjure
an enjoyable form of magic.

In the Dammed River

(The Raquette River in Northern New York has 27 power dams.)

We swim naked
in copper water
three witches
and the spell swirls
to life with our con-
juring arms.
Not far off Rough
Rock Trail and easy
to catch should
anyone try,
but we risk it for
the magic
of the current
on our skin. We bounce
and sag and
bulge, nothing like
dryads or nymphs. But
once immersed
our limbs shimmer
in this wet mirror
and trick time
beneath pine trees
perfecting August.

A Wardrobe of Stolen Dreams

I moved into someone's dream
as it sat like luggage at the airport,
waiting to be claimed. The clothes
did not fit at first or show off
my best side, but I paused, pushed
away the doubt through
afternoons of a caramel October,
until my face seemed to stay
that way, the old wives' tale
made true. Turns out
I lucked into this dream that could
have drained me, stitched me hard
inside a nightmare, but didn't,
and now I should relinquish these
stolen dreams, but I won't. Instead
I'll wait out the statute
of limitations, set my own
limits on the state
of my affairs and let myself
settle in to dreaming as it
becomes mine.

First Words

I still have cells, bits of appendix
and lung to match the young girl
at ten who perched high on
a dresser and stared out a small
rectangle of window at snow
covering the road that curved
out of sight. She was there with
pencil in hand, an impulse loose
in the world and perhaps meant
to strike her much later, when
she was old enough to understand.
But instead, she scribbled down

the snow of Thanksgiving Day

as her family made their banging,
calling house noises to one another
and the smell of turkey rose
slowly to her room. To capture
it, she sat still and listened
for the pulse of glaciers and calm,
seeping teabags, the call of tree frogs
and afternoon pink. No one had taught her
this thinking, a pause uncommon
but pure as a crocus. Decades later
that single line of words has moved
forever across a page to land in the present
and remember.

Aubade

Once my legs might have wound
like sapling roots around yours,

our radar senses seeking
just the breath of distance.

Like swooping bats through gray,
we could swing and hover,

echo-locate and attend to one another
for hours. Waking bunched

in sheets and blankets, the best of us lay
strewn like dandelion seed. But now,

most nights, only my side of the bed
peels back and opens like a tulip. Your half

remains unblossomed, a field clear-cut, left
fallow. I have worn out your soil

and you will not consider what we might
plant this late season to bring you back.

Winter Rounds

February you beat me this year
with magnetic fists and a ballerina's
precision. No glancing blow or
blown circuits, no half-dark shadows
where threads of light could dangle
and my eyes take a moment, but
adjust. No, this hammering and lustful
catastrophe held me long past
the ten count. In fact referees
called the fight while I bled and begged
on the canvas. I hope the champion's
belt is real gold, hope the victory
was worth its price. While you
may not be at fault, you could show
a little less joy in my defeat, could
offer a hand to pull me into March,
but you don't. Muscles flexed,
eyes apprised and on the prize,
you circle the ring while I crawl
toward my stool in silence.

Balance Beam

How do her toes know
to grip the beam?
Her hands hold varnished
wood, slippery wood and I
hold my breath. Wonder
again, how her body,
a body once suspended
in the fluid of my body
can now kick itself
upright on four inches of wood.
Suspended and holding, holding
holding. Feet again planted,
her very cells balance
in this twist the other way.
Like grinning soldiers on parade
her fingers, aligned
precise and yes, joyful.
Now she must tuck,
knees to chest, again
no strings, no cord. My fear
paws the ground, ready
to charge, but she stays up,
regains her surface and glides
to the dismount. I clap,
call her name, cheer
for this stranger, this daughter,
balanced without me.

Flood

In these endless days of rain
can I find a story of
excess, metaphor of damp?
Perhaps some punishment for
our profligate ways or mold
hidden in garage corners.
Each surface slick with sin,
coated in desire like panko
bread crumbs, so much tilapia
in a pan. I await
the weatherman, soothsayer
at 11, sending signs
of a weakening front,
a prevailing wind to carry
off this latest deluge.
Instead I wake, sweaty and sore
on the couch to uncover
mushrooms, sprouting their meaty
heads between my fingers,
my ears thick with stream run off.

Now I See the Drawing You Made

Your sketch of me, smudged on the ridge
by your left hand, is a curse, this course your
fingers trace, to trail a track of what I mean
to you. Sorry you say, without meaning it,
for the dulling of my eyes that I dolled for
you, the careless, careful way you show
me not to care. I learn these lessons as you
lessen your intentions. Stuck like a seed
deep in my gums, your memory takes
unruly root, breaks skin, the rules, my heart
with these strokes of charcoal on the page
when you won't even stroke my arm
as it waits beside you in the wake
of affection, the ripple I tried to call love.

The Heron

I take my son fishing
because I promised, but
I am restless, a pacing
clock counting each cast,
measuring how long I must
stay to check this off
the scrolled, sacred
list of this day's tasks.
Across the pond, on impossible
legs, she stands. Retired,
waiting. I have to look twice
to see that she is not shadow
or reeds in this cup
of afternoon light.
The flick of a tail
will come to her; trust
woven deep in the DNA
of her feathers.
What patience watches
in the shallows. Where
would I find such strength
to stop
and still myself?
Look around
with an almost imperceptible
turn of my neck?
What would in fact swim by
if any day I let myself,
for even two breaths,
stand still?

Timing

I am not good soil for anything
these days. And I remember reading
that seeds must not be planted within
two weeks of a waxing moon or they will

tunnel away and rot. What nonsense,
common sense, sixth sense gives us such beliefs?
Never plant on the thirty-first
of any month, do not wear white

after Labor Day and water pansies
only at six a.m. If you wake
at six ten, leave them dry I suppose,
since timing it seems is everything.

Trees cut or laundry hung to dry
will fester in a waxing moon,
but it's good luck to weed, mow, harvest
and kill pests in that same fourth quarter.

What hidden pulse beneath bedrock and soil
aligns us like lovers with the moon?
What we observe becomes what we believe.
What we believe becomes what we pass on.

Such timing may not be everything,
but it may be one thing or some thing.
It probably isn't   nothing.
Perhaps in the next moon, if I work

out the timing, I will not send
everything scattering out before
me, out of reach, out of time,
without nourishment or a plan.

After Rain

I stand beneath a tree
drenched; drops
collect and hang.
Another shower waiting.

This next storm surprised
from leaves, even as I trusted
the sun that makes
Adirondack summer.

Feet wet in ferns
that touch like tongues,
I move—dazzled and soaked,
on guard now.

No cover,
no reprieve,
a certainty I know
but ignore.

This shoe too will
strike while I look
to the ground,
seek luck and chanterelles,

not thinking how
one storm crouches
behind another.
And after second rain

when I dry off,
saunter off and shake out
my drowning limbs,
comes the third.

Altered Plans
for my mom

We said we would pick
raspberries—the wild ones
we saw, still green,
but swelling, near
Stone Valley in May.
By July, the bushes
must have sagged
beneath the weight
of unpicked fruit,
and birds stained their
beaks red, while you sat
in a hospital
where doctors do their
telling. I held your
hands, shaky as fledglings
dropped too soon from
a nest, and wished
for the scratches of
a raspberry patch.

Housework

I've been wondering about a trade for
sonnets—forget sparkling sinks and laundry
without wrinkles and make lines that grow sure
on my page, a record of what I see
when the mess builds around me and I choose
to leave the dirty glass, the opened mail,
cast-off shoes and my son's half-built legos
all where they fell, and trust I have not failed
but rather, selected a better way.
Can I take more risks and learn to scatter
syllables without any sense of waste?
Unmade beds cannot guarantee a cure
for the clean, empty surface of my mind,
but words might lie in the junk left behind.

North on 81

We leave suburbia the moment summer
hatches. Straight into the North Country
we rush, past Watertown, Fort Drum,
Indian River. Officially top state
and our pulse slows as the trees spread
wide. There is more space here
than sense or purpose,
more green than hope in a style at once
lovely and desperate in its decay.

Passing through here in June, one
can forget the deep coma of January,
the welfare weeks and too much
nothing in the hours of each day.
Right now, burned by affluence
and opportunity, we rebel and resist
the need to behave, believe, become
that filled each school day with failure.

We let the smell of cut grass
and splatter of may flies on the windshield
release a memory of childhood
without lessons or prospects or scores.
This trip is just what we need, an escape
from progress and plans, a fleeing really
of the lives we chose, without
knowing consequences, when we looked
only for the benefit of new, busy and highly
rated. How could we have chosen otherwise
when measuring a child's future?

We could not have known what the years would
drop on our heads like bad fruit. We can
only wish to be less impressed by flash
and glory, even though we will return,
put ourselves back in a race we can't run.
For this week however, we will sit in a boat
with little hope of a fish and let
the river rock our tired blood to sleep.

Agitating Beauty

Chinese painters say
in serenity
one can paint only
fans. A waterfall
or rising flower
stirring the air near
a fine lady's nose.

I too paint fans when
life is kind, shellac
each moment with calm
and grimace when I
make only flower-
shaped words: an orchid
rimmed in gold, blossoms
of the plum arranged
on a moon-lit pool.

Today my empty
stretch of silk awaits
some filament born
of a peace I must
shatter if the real
words can hope to spin.

Gathering

I see the wild places
on the journey of my day.
Ungroomed, untrammeled,
unwatched
until I intrude, add
my steps, my quiet eyes,
my pen. They give me,
these places, no attention,
continue long after I have left.
The bones of a beech tree
brittle and spined,
husk of a puffball
small twist of smoking
spores, a frothing spring,
some deep belly gurgle
spat from a cave
beneath roots, the red
of a leaf, new fallen
and placed by planetary
forces in the center
of a puddle black
with old rain.
These I gather, hold onto
and breathe in as I journey back.
Nothing has reached conclusion
or even change, but newly, I
will see and move in the circles
both worn and splintered.

Beth Konkoski has published poetry, fiction, and non-fiction in literary journals for more than twenty years. Her work has appeared in publications such as: *Story, Mid-American Review, The Baltimore Review,* and *New Delta Review.* Her first chapbook of poems, *Noticing the Splash,* was published by BoneWorld Press in 2010, and her work has been nominated for a Pushcart Prize and a Best of the Net Award. She is a frequent reader in the Washington D.C. area and helps coordinate the Joaquin Miller Reading Series held in Rock Creek Park each summer. She lives in Northern Virginia with her husband and two children where she teaches high school English.